Let's Cook!

PaRragon

Bath · New York · Singapore · Hong Kong · Cologne · Delhi
Melbourne · Amsterdam · Johannesburg · Auckland · Shenzhen

With special thanks to our models Sophie Collins,
Zion Doherty, Fran Eames and Kristal Lau

Home economist: Pamela Gwyther

This edition published by Parragon in 2011
Parragon
Queen Street House
4 Queen Street
Bath BA1 1HE, UK
www.parragon.com

ISBN 978-1-4454-6517-3

Printed in China

CONTENTS

THE MAGIC OF COOKING 4

COOKING TIPS 6

RECIPES 8

COOKING THINGS 46

COOKING WORDS 47

INDEX 48

THE MAGIC OF COOKING

Everyone enjoys eating delicious food, but cooking it can be even more fun. Cooking is a kind of magic. In a couple of hours you can change a piece of raw dough into a tray of warm, mouth-watering bread rolls!

To be a good cook, you need to get everything ready in the kitchen before you start. Follow the recipe steps carefully, and make sure you use your cooking equipment in the right way. Take a few minutes to read these pages, and then you'll be ready to GET COOKING!

You will find these symbols on your recipe pages:

serves 2   makes 6   preparation time   cooking time   no cooking needed   chilling time

WEIGHING AND MEASURING

- A recipe will work much better if you weigh or measure your ingredients accurately. Guessing is not a good idea!

- Use kitchen weighing scales to measure out dry ingredients such as flour and sugar.

- Use a measuring jug for liquids – make sure you place the jug on a flat surface to measure accurately.

SAFETY FIRST!

- Look out for the  symbol in the recipes. When you see this ask for adult help to:

    – move food in and out of a hot oven,
    – cook on the hob,
    – use a sharp knife,
    – use an electrical appliance such as a blender or a food processor.

- Always wear oven gloves when handling hot dishes, tins and trays.

- Remember to switch off your oven when you have finished cooking.

- When cooking on a hob, turn the pan handle to one side to avoid the heat. This also makes it harder to knock the pan off accidentally.

- Hold a saucepan handle steady with one hand while you stir.

- Always put hot pans on a heatproof mat when you remove them from the hob.

- Always chop or cut food on a chopping board, not on your work surface.

- Keep sharp knives in a knife block or a safety wrapper when not in use.

- Never walk around with a sharp knife in your hand.

- Make sure your hands are dry when plugging and unplugging electrical equipment.

- Wipe up any spills on the floor straight away.

CLEAN AND TIDY

- Always wash your hands before you start to cook. When making pastry or bread, scrub your nails clean.

- Roll up your sleeves and always wear an apron.

- Tie back your hair if it's long.

- Make sure work surfaces and equipment are clean.

- Use clean tea towels. Use a different towel to dry your hands.

- Wash your chopping board and knife in between different uses, especially after cutting up raw meat.

COOKING TIPS

Read through the recipe and make sure you have bought all the necessary ingredients. Some recipes are more difficult than others and need lots of ingredients. All the recipes in this book are graded as ★ easy ★★ medium ★★★ difficult (you may need adult help for these)

Check through the equipment list for each recipe before you start.

Here are a few useful tips about some of the basic cooking skills that you will use for the recipes in this book.

WHISKING

You whisk air into egg whites or cream to make them lighter. An electric hand mixer is a help, but a balloon whisk will also do the job.

FOLDING IN

Using a metal spoon or a plastic spatula, carefully fold one mixture into another until all the ingredients are mixed together.

RUBBING IN

When making pastry or scones, you rub the butter and flour between your fingertips until the mixture looks like breadcrumbs.

ROLLING OUT

When rolling out pastry, lightly flour the surface and the rolling pin. Roll out the pastry gently, without stretching it.

SEPARATING EGGS

Crack the shell and pour the egg onto a saucer. Place an eggcup over the yolk and pour the white into a bowl. Use the yolk as needed.

LINING A TIN

Line the tin with baking paper when making cakes, brownies or flapjacks. It stops the cakes sticking to the tin.

MELTING

When melting chocolate, make sure the bottom of the bowl doesn't touch the water in the pan. If the chocolate gets too hot, it will be spoiled!

KNEADING

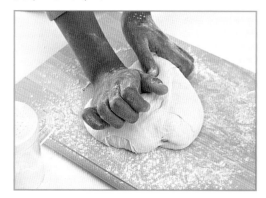

You knead bread dough to make it stretchy so it will hold in air when cooking. Pull and stretch the dough with your hands until smooth.

serves 8

30 minutes

no cooking

Equipment

- chopping board
- sharp knife
- mixing bowl
- wooden spoon
- food processor
- tablespoon
- serving plate
- 2 small bowls
- measuring jug

STICKS AND DIPS ⭐

Crudités are fab finger food — great for lunch boxes, parties or just when you have the munchies! Chunky sticks of raw vegetables with dreamy flavoured dips — m'mmmm!

What you need:

Crudités

4 carrots, peeled

2 courgettes

4 sticks of celery

half a cucumber

1 red pepper

1 yellow pepper

8 baby sweetcorn

Cheesy Dip

250 g cream cheese

2 tbsp milk

2 spring onions, finely chopped

1 tbsp freshly chopped parsley

1 tbsp chives

salt and freshly ground black pepper

Hummus

400 g canned chickpeas, drained

juice of 1 lemon

2 cloves of garlic, crushed

2 tbsp tahini (sesame paste)

125 ml olive oil

salt and freshly ground black pepper

freshly chopped parsley and paprika to garnish

CHEESY DIP

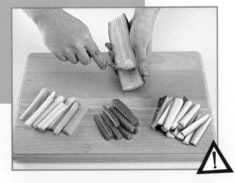

1. Cut the carrots, courgettes and celery into sticks 6 cm long. Halve the cucumber, remove the seeds and cut into equal-sized sticks.

2. Halve the peppers and remove the seeds. Cut each half into long strips.

3. Make the cheesy dip by mixing the cheese and milk until smooth. Add the other ingredients and season.

Hummus

4. Blend the chickpeas, lemon juice and garlic in the processor. Add the tahini and blend until smooth.

5. Keep the machine running and add the oil, a little at a time. Season.

6. Put the dip and hummus in small bowls. Sprinkle hummus with parsley and paprika. Put the bowls on a serving plate with the crudités around them.

makes 4

15 minutes

70–90 minutes

Equipment

- fork
- baking tray
- dessert spoon
- mixing bowl
- sharp knife
- chopping board
- grater

JACKET POTATOES ★★

For a cosy evening at home, hot jacket potatoes are a brilliant meal. You can stuff them with your favourite fillings and eat them piping hot from the oven!

What you need:

4 large potatoes, about 250 g each

55 g butter

salt and freshly ground black pepper

115 g ham

115 g Cheddar cheese

For a change!

For a veggie option try some fried mushrooms instead of the ham.

Add flaked canned tuna or salmon to the mashed potato instead of ham.

For an extra tasty meal, halve the hot potatoes and pour over some minced chilli sauce or bolognese sauce. Sprinkle with cheese to finish.

1. Preheat the oven to 200°C/gas mark 6. Wash and wipe the potatoes. Prick with a fork and place on a baking tray.

2. Cook the potatoes in the oven for 60–75 minutes until they are soft inside and the skins are crisp. Remove them from the oven.

3. Cut each potato in half and scoop out the soft insides into the mixing bowl. Take care not to damage the skins.

4. Mash the potato well with the fork. Add the butter and season.

5. Place the skins on the baking tray. Chop the ham and put some into each shell. Spoon in the potato.

6. Grate the cheese and sprinkle on the potatoes. Put them back in the oven and cook for a further 15 minutes until the tops are golden.

serves 4

20–25 minutes

20–25 minutes

PASTA BAKE

For a delicious dinner, pasta is the ultimate yummy food. A pasta bake is a brilliant way to make large amounts of food to feed all your friends. They'll love the gorgeous sauce and crunchy topping!

Equipment

- large saucepan
- medium saucepan
- wooden spatula
- grater
- colander
- ovenproof dish
- baking tray
- measuring jug

What you need:

250 g pasta shapes

¼ tsp salt

55 g butter

40 g plain flour

450 ml milk

125 g Cheddar cheese, grated

125 g cooked ham, roughly chopped

4 cherry tomatoes, cut into quarters

salt and freshly ground black pepper

25 g Parmesan cheese, freshly grated

For a change!

Add 115 g sweetcorn and 220 g canned tuna, drained and flaked, to the pasta.

1. Preheat the oven to 200°C/ gas mark 6. Heat some water in the large saucepan. Add salt and bring to the boil.

2. Add the pasta carefully, taking care not to splash. Cook the pasta according to the pack instructions.

3. Gently melt the butter in a saucepan over a low heat. Add the flour and mix well. Cook mixture for 1 minute and then remove from heat.

4. Stir in the milk, a little at a time, to make a smooth sauce. Put pan back on heat. Stir while the sauce thickens so it doesn't go lumpy.

5. When the sauce boils, turn down heat and cook, stirring, for 1–2 minutes. Remove from heat. Mix in the Cheddar, ham and tomatoes. Season.

6. Drain the pasta. Mix with the sauce. Place in ovenproof dish and sprinkle with Parmesan. Bake in oven, on a baking tray, for 20–25 minutes.

makes 4–6

15 minutes + 10 minutes for chilling

10–12 minutes

Equipment

- mixing bowl
- fork
- chopping board
- sharp knife
- grill pan
- foil
- pastry brush
- cooking tongs

BEST-EVER BURGERS

You can have a fab time making these tasty burgers using both meat and vegetables. Make them even more yummy by adding your favourite sauce!

What you need:

450 g minced beef

1 onion, finely chopped

1 egg, beaten

salt and freshly ground black pepper

1 tbsp flour for shaping

1 tbsp olive oil

To Serve

4–6 burger buns

half a lettuce

2 tomatoes

mustard, ketchup or mayonnaise

For a change!

To make veggie burgers, you will need:

2 400-g cans of cannellini beans, drained and rinsed
2 tbsp chopped parsley or coriander
grated rind of 1 lemon
1 beaten egg

Mix together in a blender. Season well and shape the mixture into 4 even-sized burgers. Chill for 1–2 hours and then fry in a non-stick frying pan for 5 minutes on each side. Serve with salad.

1. Put the mince in the mixing bowl and add the onion, egg and seasoning. Mix well.

2. Lightly flour your hands and the chopping board. Divide the mixture into 4–6 equal portions and shape into burgers.

3. Chill the burgers in the fridge for 10 minutes. Preheat the grill. Place the chilled burgers on the grill pan and brush with oil.

4. Grill the burgers for 4–6 minutes. Turn the burgers over, brush again with oil. Grill for a further 4–6 minutes until done.

5. Cut the buns in half. Toast them under the hot grill if you wish. Slice the tomatoes thinly. Wash and shred the lettuce.

6. Place a handful of lettuce in each bun, then add the burger and a slice of tomato. Serve with your own choice of sauce.

makes 8

20 minutes
+ rising

10–15 minutes

BREAD ROLLS

Home-made bread rolls are a special treat. Nothing smells better than fresh bread straight from the oven. It's fun to make and delicious to eat!

What you need:

450 g strong white flour

1 tsp salt

1 x 7-g sachet easy-blend yeast

1 tbsp vegetable oil

350 ml warm water

2 tbsp flour for dusting

1 egg, beaten, for glazing

sesame or poppy seeds to decorate

Equipment

- large mixing bowl
- wooden spoon
- measuring jug
- flour shaker
- chopping board
- clingfilm
- knife
- baking sheet
- pastry brush
- cooling rack
- tea towel

For a change!

Use half white and half wholemeal flour to make brown rolls.

Cook's tip!

To test that your bread is cooked, tap the base of each roll – you should hear a hollow sound.

Remember to cool your rolls before eating them!

1. Mix the flour, salt and yeast in a bowl. Add the oil and water. Stir to form a soft dough.

2. Knead dough on a floured surface for 5–7 minutes until smooth and elastic. Place in the bowl, cover with clingfilm and leave in a warm place.

3. When the dough has doubled in size (about 1 hour), knead it again on a lightly floured surface until smooth. Divide into 8 equal pieces.

4. Shape half the dough into round buns. Make the other half into cottage rolls with a small round shape on top. Place on a baking sheet.

5. Cover rolls with a tea towel. Leave to rise for 30 minutes, until the bread has doubled in size. Preheat oven to 220°C/ gas mark 7.

6. Glaze the rolls with egg and decorate with seeds. Sprinkle with flour for a soft bap. Bake in oven for 10–15 minutes until golden brown.

serves 4

15 minutes +
1 hour marinating

5–6 minutes

Equipment

- sharp knife
- chopping board
- non-metallic dish
- wooden spoon
- clingfilm
- bowl
- fork
- frying pan
- slotted spoon
- large serving plate
- 2 small bowls

SPICY WRAPS

Fajitas taste sensational! They come from Mexico and are soft tortillas filled with meat, salad and some spicy sauce. You'll have a fab time making them!

what you need:

1 red and 1 yellow pepper

2 skinless chicken breast fillets

2 tbsp olive oil

2 tsp mild chilli powder

1 tsp paprika

juice and grated rind of 1 lime

salt and freshly ground black pepper

4 soft flour tortillas

55 g shredded iceberg lettuce

4 tbsp soured cream or plain yoghurt

Spicy Tomato and Avocado Sauce

2 tomatoes, deseeded and chopped

1 small red onion, very finely chopped

1 tbsp lime juice

1 tbsp olive oil

1 avocado, peeled, stoned and diced

1 tbsp chopped fresh coriander

1. Halve the peppers, remove the seeds and cut into long strips. Cut the chicken fillets into strips and place in a non-metallic dish.

2. Add half the oil, the spices and lime juice and rind. Season. Cover and leave in the fridge for 1 hour.

3. To make the spicy tomato sauce, mix together all the ingredients. Season, cover and keep cool.

4. Heat the remaining oil in a frying pan. Fry the chicken, stirring, for 3 minutes. Add the peppers and fry for 3 minutes, until the chicken is cooked.

5. Remove pan from heat. Spoon out the chicken and peppers and keep warm. Heat the tortillas in the oven. Put the sauce and cream in bowls.

6. To make your fajita, put some sauce and sour cream onto a tortilla. Add the chicken, peppers and lettuce. Roll up your fajita and eat it!

For a change!

Use cooked minced beef instead of chicken.

For a veggie option, use grated cheese instead of chicken or beef.

makes 8

15 minutes
+1 hour marinating

8–10 minutes

FAB KEBABS

Kebabs make a wicked snack at any time, but they're particularly good in the summer when they can be cooked on a barbecue. These instructions are for cooking under the grill, but the kebabs will taste just as yummy!

Equipment

- tablespoon
- mixing bowl
- lemon squeezer
- garlic crusher
- sharp knife
- chopping board
- slotted spoon
- plate
- clingfilm and foil
- 8 wooden skewers
- pastry brush
- cooking tongs

What you need:

Marinade

4 tbsp olive oil

juice of 1 lemon

1 clove of garlic, crushed

salt and freshly ground black pepper

Kebabs

450 g boned leg of lamb

2 red onions

8 mushrooms

8 cherry tomatoes

8 bay leaves

For a change!

Prawns and cubes of salmon can be used to make tasty fish kebabs.

To make veggie kebabs, use onions, squares of red and yellow pepper, chunks of courgettes and aubergines, boiled new potatoes and whole small tomatoes. Add some honey to the marinade for extra tastiness!

1. Mix together the marinade ingredients in a bowl. Cut the meat into 2-cm cubes.

2. Add the meat to the bowl and stir well. Cover and put in the fridge for 1–2 hours. Remove meat from the bowl onto a plate.

3. Peel the onions and cut into chunky wedges. Wash the tomatoes. Wipe the mushrooms. Soak the skewers in cold water for 30 minutes.

4. Push alternate meat cubes, onions, mushrooms, tomatoes and bay leaves onto the skewers. (Take care not to prick your fingers.)

5. Preheat the grill. Line the grill pan with foil. Place the kebabs on the grill pan and brush with the marinade.

6. Grill for 8–10 minutes. Turn the kebabs every 2 minutes to make sure they are cooked evenly. Serve with salad and rice or a jacket potato.

makes 2 (serves 4)

15 minutes
plus rising

15–20 minutes

Equipment

- large mixing bowl
- wooden spoon
- measuring jug
- flour shaker
- chopping board
- rolling pin
- clingfilm
- knife
- 2 baking sheets (greased)
- sieve
- bowl

PIZZAS TO GO!

In a lazy mood but feeling hungry? Then pizza is a brilliant idea for a fun, easy meal. Making your own pizzas is loads of floury fun — and if you make these mini ones everyone can choose their own tasty topping.

What you need:

Base

225 g strong white flour

$\frac{1}{2}$ tsp salt

2 tsp easy-blend yeast

1 tbsp vegetable oil

175 ml warm water

2 tbsp flour for dusting

Topping

400 g canned chopped tomatoes

2 tbsp tomato purée

2 tsp dried oregano

salt and freshly ground black pepper

2 slices of ham, torn into bite-sized pieces

150 g mozzarella, torn into bite-sized pieces

1 yellow pepper, sliced

4 button mushrooms, sliced

2 tbsp olive oil

1. Make the dough following the instructions for bread on page 16, up to the end of step 3.

2. Flour your hands and the work surface. Knead the dough until smooth. Stretch into shape and roll thinly into two circles, 15 cm across.

3. Pinch up the edges of the dough. Grease the baking sheets. Place the bases on the sheets and leave them to rise while you make the topping.

4. Preheat the oven to 220°C/gas mark 7. Drain the tomatoes and put into a bowl with the purée and oregano. Mix and season.

5. Spread half the mixture over each base. Arrange the ham, cheese, pepper and mushrooms on top. Brush over the olive oil.

6. Bake in the oven for 15–20 minutes until the crusts are pale golden and firm. Remove from the oven and serve.

makes 12

25 minutes

15–20 minutes

Equipment

- mixing bowl
- sieve
- tablespoon
- fork
- round-bladed knife
- flour shaker
- rolling pin
- 7.5-cm pastry cutter
- bun tin
- measuring jug
- small frying pan
- wooden spatula
- cooling rack

TASTY TARTS

You'll have a fab time making these easy-peasy tasty tarts. Get creative with your choice of fillings — anything goes! Don't forget that you can make sweet tarts too!

What you need:

175 g plain flour

pinch of salt

85 g butter (or a mixture of butter and vegetable shortening)

2–3 tbsp cold water to mix

2 rashers of bacon, chopped into small pieces

2 eggs, beaten

60 g grated Cheddar cheese

150 ml milk

salt and freshly ground pepper

For a change!

For a veggie option, fry some sliced leeks and place in the cases before adding the egg mixture.

Make jam tarts using red jam or lemon curd, or try open mince pies with mincemeat.

1. Preheat the oven to 200°C/gas mark 6. Sieve the flour and salt into the bowl. Add the butter and rub it into the flour. It should look like breadcrumbs.

2. Sprinkle on the water and stir the mixture with a knife to make it come together. Press the pastry into a ball — the bowl should be clean.

3. On a lightly floured surface slightly flatten the pastry with your hand. Then roll out to form a rough circle about 3 mm thick.

24

4. Cut out the pastry circles and place in the bun tin.

5. Fry the bacon in a frying pan until crisp. Mix together the eggs, cheese, bacon, milk and seasoning.

6. Spoon the mixture into the cases. Bake in the oven for 15 minutes. Remove from the oven. Leave to cool slightly and then place on a wire rack.

serves 2

25 minutes

40–50 minutes

Equipment

- cook's knife
- chopping board
- plate
- bowl
- fork
- shallow dish
- plastic bag
- 2 baking trays
- pastry brush
- cooking tongs
- fish slice

CHUNKY FISH AND CHIPS ★★★

Wow! With this funky recipe you can make your very own take-away food at home. The fish is coated with breadcrumbs, giving it the crunchiest, crumbliest coating!

what you need:

2 fillets of plaice or other white fish, skinned and cut into 1-cm-wide strips

salt and pepper

2 tbsp plain flour

1 egg

115 g white or wholemeal breadcrumbs

1 tbsp finely chopped fresh parsley

2 large potatoes, scrubbed

6 tbsp olive oil

To Serve

half a lemon, cut into segments

ketchup or mayonnaise

1. Preheat the oven to 200°C/gas mark 6. Season the flour and put on a plate. Roll the strips of fish in the flour until covered.

2. Beat the egg in a bowl and pour it into a shallow dish. Dip the fish into the beaten egg. Mix the parsley and breadcrumbs. Season.

3. Put the mixture into a plastic bag and toss in the fish to coat thoroughly. Chill on a baking tray in the fridge for 30 minutes.

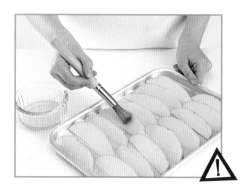  

4. Cut each potato into 8 wedges. Place on a baking tray and brush over half the oil. Turn the potatoes and brush the other side. Season.

5. Bake the chips for 35–40 minutes until golden, turning occasionally. After 20 minutes remove the fish from fridge. Drizzle with the rest of the oil.

6. Bake at the top of the oven for 15–20 minutes, turning halfway through. Serve with the lemon and your favourite sauce.

makes 10

5 minutes

15–20 minutes

PERFECT PANCAKES ★★★

Why wait for Pancake Day? These tasty treats can be mixed up in moments at any time. You can add anything you like as a topping — from sugar, maple syrup or honey with lemon juice to lashings of chocolate sauce!

Equipment

- sieve
- mixing bowl
- wooden spoon
- measuring jug
- 18-cm non-stick frying pan
- wooden spatula
- baking paper

What you need:

100 g plain flour

pinch of salt

1 egg, beaten

300 ml milk

10 tsp butter or oil

To Serve

lemon juice

caster sugar

For a change!

Serve your pancakes with warmed honey or jam. Or try them with sliced bananas and runny chocolate sauce.

Go savoury and layer up the pancakes with meat or vegetable fillings. Serve with a topping of melted grated cheese.

1. Sieve the flour and salt into the bowl. Make a 'well' in the centre; add the egg and half the milk. Beat the egg and milk together.

2. Gradually mix in the flour. When the mixture is smooth with no lumps, beat in the rest of the milk. Carefully pour the mixture into the jug.

3. Heat the pan over a medium heat. Add a teaspoon of the butter or oil and swirl it around to cover the whole surface.

4. Pour in enough batter to cover the base. Swirl around the pan while tilting it so you have a thin, even layer. Cook for about 30 seconds.

5. Lift up the edge of the pancake to see if it is brown. Loosen round the edges and flip with the spatula. Cook the other side until golden brown.

6. Turn out each pancake onto a warm plate. Stack in layers with baking paper. Cover with foil and keep warm.

Serve them hot!

Serve the pancakes while they're still hot. Sprinkle with the lemon juice and sugar and roll them up.

makes 12

20 minutes

1 hour for chilling

CHOCOLATE CRISPIES ★

This is an easy-peasy recipe – probably one of the very first recipes you'll make. These scrunchy, chewy little cakes are delicious at any time – and they need almost no cooking.

Equipment

- mixing bowl
- large saucepan
- wooden spoon
- dessertspoon
- knife
- bun tin
- 12 paper cases

what you need:

55 g butter

4 tbsp golden syrup

100 g milk chocolate, broken into pieces

70 g cornflakes

For a change!

You can use puffed wheat or rice crispies instead of the cornflakes.

You could use dark chocolate or even white if you like. Add 55 g raisins to make even chewier crispie cakes.

1. Put the butter, syrup and chocolate in the mixing bowl. Place the bowl over a large saucepan of simmering water.

2. Allow the butter, syrup and chocolate to melt, stirring to mix well.

3. Remove the pan from the heat. Take the bowl out of the saucepan.

4. Add the cornflakes to the mixture and stir well, using a wooden spoon.

5. Carefully spoon the mixture into the paper cases. Take care you don't make the cases too messy.

6. Leave your crispies to set in the fridge for 1 hour. You can store them in an airtight tin so they stay crisp.

makes 24

30 minutes

1 hour for
chilling

Equipment

- mixing bowl
- balloon whisk
- sieve
- wooden spoon
- chopping board
- teaspoon
- baking tray lined
  with non-stick paper
- fork
- small saucepan
- heatproof bowl

PEPPERMINT CREAMS ★

These scrummy peppermint creams make great presents for mums, dads, grandparents — even best friends. They are easy to make, and you'll have fun dipping them in the chocolate. Don't eat all the sweets while making them!

What you need:

1 egg white

350 g white icing sugar
+ extra for shaping

3 drops peppermint essence

2 drops green food colouring

125 g dark chocolate,
broken into pieces

Gift Wrapped

Arrange your peppermint creams in a prettily decorated box or tin lined with coloured tissue paper. Your granny or teacher will love them!

1. Whisk the egg white until frothy. Sieve in the icing sugar and mix well. Add the peppermint essence and the colouring and mix well.

2. Sprinkle icing sugar onto your hands. Roll teaspoon-sized amounts of the mixture into small balls and place on the baking tray.

3. Flatten each ball with a fork to form flat discs. Place in the fridge for 1 hour until firm.

4. Put the chocolate pieces into the heatproof bowl. Place the bowl on the pan of simmering water (about 5 cm deep).

5. When the chocolate has melted, remove from the heat and stir until smooth. Allow to cool a little.

6. Dip each sweet into the chocolate until half covered. Place sweets on the non-stick paper to set. Keep in a cool place or a fridge until needed.

makes about 18

10–15 minutes

25–30 minutes

Equipment

- rectangular cake tin 20 x 30 cm, greased and lined with baking paper
- large saucepan
- wooden spoon
- flexible spatula
- round-bladed knife
- cooling rack
- cake tin for storage

MUNCHY FLAPJACKS ★ ★

Flapjacks are a really scrummy treat for when you have the munchies! They taste great and, as they are made from oats, they're good for you too!

What you need:

175 g butter

125 g soft light-brown sugar

55 g golden syrup

350 g porridge oats

For a change!

You can add 70 g raisins to make fruity flapjacks. For an extra-healthy option, add 55 g chopped dates and 55 g sunflower seeds. Try using honey instead of syrup.

For a fab treat, melt 55 g dark chocolate and dip the flapjacks in to coat the top. Cool on a wire rack while the chocolate sets.

1. Preheat the oven to 180°C/gas mark 4. Put the butter, sugar and syrup into the saucepan.

2. Heat pan over a low heat for 2–3 minutes, stirring until melted. Remove the pan from the hob, add the porridge oats and mix.

3. Pour the mixture into the prepared cake tin. Press down well using a spatula.

4. Bake in the centre of the oven for 25–30 minutes until golden but still slightly soft. Remove from the oven and leave to cool for 10 minutes.

5. Cut into squares and allow to cool completely in the tin.

6. Carefully remove the flapjacks from the tin using a knife. Store in an airtight container for up to 1 week.

makes 18

15 minutes

15–20 minutes

MINI COOKIES

These bite-sized delights are great snacks.
The only problem is that everyone will love them,
so don't be surprised if they all get eaten
very quickly!

Equipment

- mixing bowl
- wooden spoon or electric hand mixer
- small bowl
- fork
- sieve
- flexible spatula
- dessert spoon
- 2 baking trays lined with baking paper
- round-bladed knife
- cooling rack
- cake tin for storage

What you need:

125 g butter

125 g golden caster sugar

1 large egg, beaten

1 ripe banana, mashed

175 g self-raising flour

1 tsp mixed spice

2 tbsp milk

100 g chocolate cut into chunks

55 g raisins

For a change!

You can replace the chocolate with 100 g of chopped mixed nuts.

Make dreamy peanut butter cookies by adding 2 tablespoons of peanut butter instead of the banana. Use chopped peanuts instead of the chocolate. Leave out the spice and raisins.

1. Preheat the oven to 190°C/ gas mark 5. Cream together the butter and sugar with a wooden spoon or mixer until light and fluffy.

2. Add the egg gradually to the mixture, beating well each time. Mash the banana and add it in, beating until the mixture is smooth.

3. Sieve in the flour and spice. Fold in using a spatula. Add the milk to give a soft consistency. Fold in the chocolate and fruit.

4. Drop dessert spoons of the mixture onto the lined baking trays. Space cookies well apart (about 9 on each tray).

5. Bake in the centre of the oven for 15–20 minutes until lightly golden.

6. Remove from the oven and leave to firm up slightly. Transfer to a cooling rack using a round-bladed knife. Allow to cool before storing.

makes 12

20 minutes

15–20 minutes

Equipment

- mixing bowl
- wooden spoon
- sieve
- tablespoon
- muffin tin
- 12 paper cases
- dessertspoon
- cooling rack
- small bowl
- lemon squeezer

CUPCAKE TREATS ★ ★ ★

with their soft sponge middles and yummy icing topping, cupcakes are an all-time favourite teatime treat. You can make them any colour and decorate them in a funky way!

What you need:

125 g butter (softened at room temperature)

125 g caster sugar

2 eggs, beaten

125 g self-raising flour

2 tbsp milk

Icing

225 g icing sugar

1 tbsp lemon juice

1 tbsp warm water

To decorate

sweets, chocolate buttons, hundreds and thousands, silver balls, grated coconut and glacé cherries

For a change!

You can make some funky colours of icing for your cupcakes. Divide the icing mixture into small bowls and add a different colour to each one.

1. Preheat the oven to 190°C/gas mark 5. Use a wooden spoon to cream the butter and sugar until light and fluffy.

2. Add the eggs a little at a time, beating well after each addition. Sieve the flour into the bowl and carefully fold in using a tablespoon.

3. Mix in the milk. Stir until the mixture is smooth and drops off the spoon easily. Divide the mixture between the paper cases (in the tin).

4. Bake in the oven for 15–20 minutes until the cakes are risen and golden brown. Remove from the oven and put on a cooling rack.

5. Sieve the icing sugar into the bowl. Add the lemon juice and stir in the warm water. Mix until thick and smooth.

6. Spoon the icing onto the cakes. Spread to the case edges with the back of a teaspoon. Use your imagination to decorate!

makes 6

30–40 minutes

1–2 hours

GORGEOUS TRIFLE ★★★

With lashings of yummy custard and cream, trifle is a wicked treat for special days. You can add almost anything you like for a tasty topping sensation — m'mmmmmm!

Equipment

- chopping board
- sharp knife
- mixing bowl
- balloon whisk
- clingfilm
- saucepan
- wooden spoon
- measuring jug
- 6 glass bowls

What you need:

1 jam Swiss roll or 8 trifle sponges and 100 g strawberry jam

125 ml orange juice (or juice from a can of fruit)

40 g macaroons or ratafias

350 g fresh strawberries or other fruit (fresh or canned)

Custard
5 egg yolks
3 tbsp caster sugar
1/2 tsp vanilla extract
425 ml single cream

Topping
300 ml double cream
2 tbsp milk
chocolate flakes to decorate

1. Cut the sponges into pieces and spread with the jam (or just slice the Swiss roll). Place in the bowls and pour over the fruit juice.

2. Add the macaroons to the bowls and spoon the fruit on top. Cream together the egg yolks, sugar and vanilla extract in a jug.

3. Heat the single cream in a saucepan until just before boiling point. Pour the hot cream into the jug, stirring all the time until mixed.

4. Put the mixture back into the pan. Heat gently, stirring constantly, until the sauce has thickened enough to coat the back of a spoon.

5. Put the base of the pan in cold water and stir until cool. Spoon the custard over the trifle. Cover with clingfilm and leave for 1–2 hours.

6. Just before serving, whip the double cream with the milk until it is thick but soft. Spoon over the custard. Decorate and serve chilled.

makes 4

15–20 minutes

2 hours for
chilling

MEGA CHOCOLATE MOUSSE

This mousse is lots of fun to make – and it's totally delicious!
You can learn how to melt chocolate and whisk egg whites
while making a really groovy pud at the same time!

Equipment

- heatproof bowl
- saucepan
- tablespoon
- mixing bowl
- saucer
- eggcup
- small bowl
- teaspoon
- electric hand mixer or balloon whisk
- flexible spatula
- grater
- 4 small serving dishes

What you need:

125 g plain chocolate,
broken into pieces

4 large eggs

50 g white chocolate

For a change!

*For a zingy 'chocolate orange'
flavour, add grated orange
zest to the melted chocolate.*

*For a crunchy surprise, put
some chopped nuts in the
bottom of the dishes.*

1. Put the chocolate in the
heatproof bowl. Place the bowl
on a pan of simmering water
(5 cm deep) and allow the
chocolate to melt.

2. Separate the eggs following
the method described on page
7. Pour the egg whites into the
mixing bowl and put the yolks
in the small bowl.

3. Remove the melted
chocolate from the heat and
stir well. Cool a little. Beat the
yolks and slowly add them to
the chocolate, stirring well.

4. Whisk the egg whites in the mixing bowl until they are white and firm and will stand up in soft peaks.

5. With the spatula, gently fold the whites into the chocolate and egg yolk mixture until evenly mixed.

6. Carefully pour the mousse into the serving dishes and leave to set in the fridge for 2 hours. Decorate with grated white chocolate.

serves 4

5 minutes

no cooking

FUNKY FRUIT SMOOTHIES ★

Check out these delicious fruit smoothies, which you can mix up in minutes. Simply choose any of your favourite fruits and get creative with different mixtures to make some really zany drinks!

Equipment

- chopping board
- sharp knife
- blender or food processor
- measuring jug
- teaspoon

What you need:

Berry Smoothie

1 small banana

150 g fresh raspberries and strawberries

300 ml milk

caster sugar if required

Yoghurt Smoothie

1 small banana

1 ripe pear

200 ml apple juice

200 ml natural yoghurt

1 tsp vanilla extract

1 tbsp runny honey

BERRY SMOOTHIE

1. For the berry smoothie, slice the banana. Halve the strawberries if they are very large.

2. Place the fruit in the blender. Pour in the milk. Make sure the lid is on tight and blend until smooth.

3. Taste and add sugar if required. Pour into smoothie glasses and serve with straws.

YOGHURT SMOOTHIE

1. For the yoghurt smoothie, slice the banana. Peel, core and chop the pear.

2. Place all the ingredients in the blender. Make sure the lid is on tight and blend until smooth.

3. Pour into smoothie glasses and serve.

For a change!

You can add crushed ice or ice cream to your smoothie to make a cooler drink for hot summer days.

COOKING THINGS

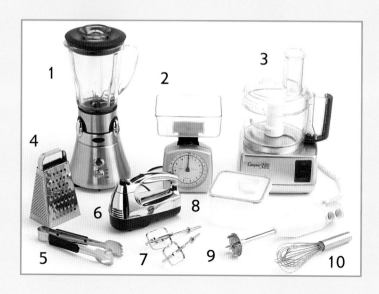

1 electric blender
2 scales
3 food processor
4 grater
5 tongs
6 electric hand mixer

7 beaters
8 freezer box
9 electric hand blender
10 balloon whisk

1 saucepans
2 colander
3 cake tin
4 bun tin
5 baking sheet
6 mixing bowl

7 sieve
8 measuring jug
9 lemon squeezer
10 rolling pin
11 oven gloves
12 cooling rack

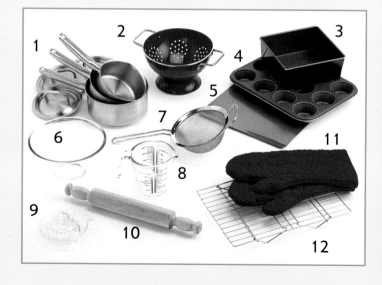

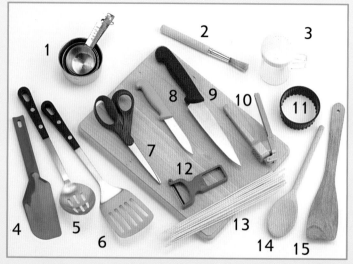

1 measuring cups
2 pastry brush
3 flour shaker
4 plastic spatula
5 slotted spoon
6 fish slice
7 scissors
8 sharp knives

9 chopping board
10 garlic crusher
11 pastry cutter
12 vegetable peeler
13 wooden skewers
14 wooden spoon
15 wooden spatula

COOKING WORDS

beat
To mix ingredients together, using a wooden spoon or hand mixer, until soft and stretchy.

blend
To mix together, using a blender or food processor, to make a liquid or a smooth mix.

chop
To chop food into small pieces with a knife.

cream
To beat butter and sugar together using a wooden spoon or hand mixer; the creamed mixture should be smooth and pale.

drain
To pour off water from cooked foods, using a sieve or a colander.

drizzle
To pour a trickle over the top of food.

fold in
To mix gently; use a metal spoon or spatula so that you don't remove the air beaten in earlier.

garnish
To decorate a savoury dish with whole or chopped herbs, chopped nuts, sliced tomatoes and so on.

glaze
To brush dough with egg yolk or milk so that it looks shiny and golden when baked.

grease
To brush a baking tray or cake tin with oil or rub with butter to stop the food from sticking.

knead
To work with bread dough on a board so that it becomes smooth and elastic.

rise
To put bread dough in a warm place so the yeast can work. The dough should double in size.

rub in
To rub butter into flour, using the tips of your fingers, to produce a mixture that looks like breadcrumbs.

season
To add salt and pepper to food to increase its taste.

sieve
To use a sieve to drain liquid or to remove any lumps from sugar or flour before adding them to a mixture; sieving also adds air to the mix.

simmer
To cook a liquid in a pan so that it bubbles gently but does not boil.

whisk
To beat a mixture very hard to add air so that the mixture becomes thick. Use either a balloon whisk or an electric hand mixer.

INDEx

bacon and ham
  jacket potatoes 10–11
  pasta bake 12–13
  pizza 22–23
  tartlets 24–25
bananas
  cookies 36–37
  fruit smoothies 44–45
beef burgers 14–15
bread rolls 16–17
burgers 14–15

cheese
  cheesy dip 8,9
  jacket potatoes 10–11
  pasta bake 12–13
  pizza 22–23
  tartlets 24–25
chicken
  fajitas 18–19
chocolate
  crispie cakes 30–31
  mousse 42–43
  peppermint creams 32–33
cleanliness 5
cookies 36–37
cooking equipment 46
crispie cakes 30–31
crudités 8–9
cupcakes 38–39

dips 8–9

eggs
  chocolate mousse 42–43
  separating and whisking 7
  tartlets 24–25

fajitas 18–19
fish and chips 26–27
flapjacks 34–35
folding in 7, 47
fruit
  smoothies 44–45
  trifle 40–41

hummus 8, 9

jam tarts 24

kebabs 20–21
kneading 7, 16, 47
knives 5

lamb kebabs 20–21
lining a tin 7

measuring 4
mince pies 24
mousse, chocolate 42–43
mushrooms
  kebabs 20–21
  pizza 22–23

nuts
  chocolate mousse 42–43
  cookies 36–37

pancakes 28–29
pasta bake 12–13
peppermint creams 32–33
peppers
  crudités 8–9
  fajitas 18–19
  pizza 22–23
pizza 22–23

potatoes
  chips 26–27
  jacket 10–11
rolling out 6
rubbing in 7, 47

safety 5
smoothies 44–45
sweetcorn
  crudités 8–9
  pasta bake 12
symbols 4

tarts
  savoury tartlets 24–25
  sweet tartlets 24
tomatoes
  fajitas 18–19
  kebabs 20–21
  pasta bake 12–13
  pizza 22–23
tortillas 18–19
trifle 40–41
tuna
  pasta bake 12–13

weighing and measuring 4
whisking 7, 47
wraps, spicy 18–19

yoghurt
  smoothies 44, 45